This book belongs to:

_____

ALLAH

made us all

different

"BE YOURSELF"

by Rabia Gelgi

Once upon a time,
there was a bird living in a
beautiful forest.

Her name was Little Birdie.

But Little Birdie was
        not really happy
            about what she was.

One day, she saw a pretty kitten
while she was flying.
Little birdie wished she was a cat too!

She landed on the ground and tried to walk
like a cat. But she only had two feet!

That's okay, thought Birdie,
"I can use my wings instead"

After a short while, her wings started to get sore, and
she wasn't able to follow the cat anymore.
She started crying,
thinking it was so difficult to be a cat.

Little Birdie gave up on being a cat
and started flying again.

This time, she saw a gorgeous butterfly who
was flying from flower to flower.

"I wonder if I look as beautiful as that butterfly
if I dye my wings!"
she thought,

and decided to paint her wings.

She did change the color of her wings
but they didn't look pretty at all.

Little birdie was so sad.

Little birdie gave up being a butterfly.

Then, she saw that there were a lot of fish swimming
at sea so peacefully that
she immediately wanted to be one of them.

However, there was this one thing she forgot; she didn't know how to **swim!**

She got out of breath when she dived into the sea.

"Oh **ALLAH!** please! help me!, help me!"
she screamed.

Alhamdulillah,
she remembered that she could fly and
she managed to save herself from the water.

She was so scared!

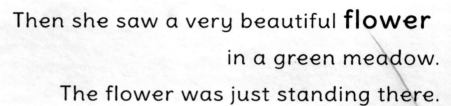

After getting some rest, she started flying again.

Then she saw a very beautiful **flower**
in a green meadow.
The flower was just standing there.

Little birdie thought that it would
be so easy to be a flower.

She perched on a branch, spread
her wings and began to stand
still as if she was a flower.

Little Birdie got too hot under the sun
and her wings got **tired** quickly.

She finally gave up being a flower and
lied down on the branch to get some **rest**.

She headed back **home** just before sunset.

Little Birdie saw an **owl** when
she was trying to sleep.

She perched on a branch right next
to the owl and kept her eyes wide
open looking around just like the owl.

How hard it was to stay awake **all night!**

Little Birdie felt exhausted!

She fell **asleep** before the sunrise.
She was still sleeping
when her friends came at noon.

When she woke up, her mom told her
"Oh sweetie **Allah** created various animals, numerous
creatures in this world, and made us all **different**. What
makes us unique is being ourselves,
and doing what we do **best**."

Little Birdie agreed and said "Trying to be someone else is
very,very hard anyway mom." Her mom smiled
and gave her a big feathery **hug**.

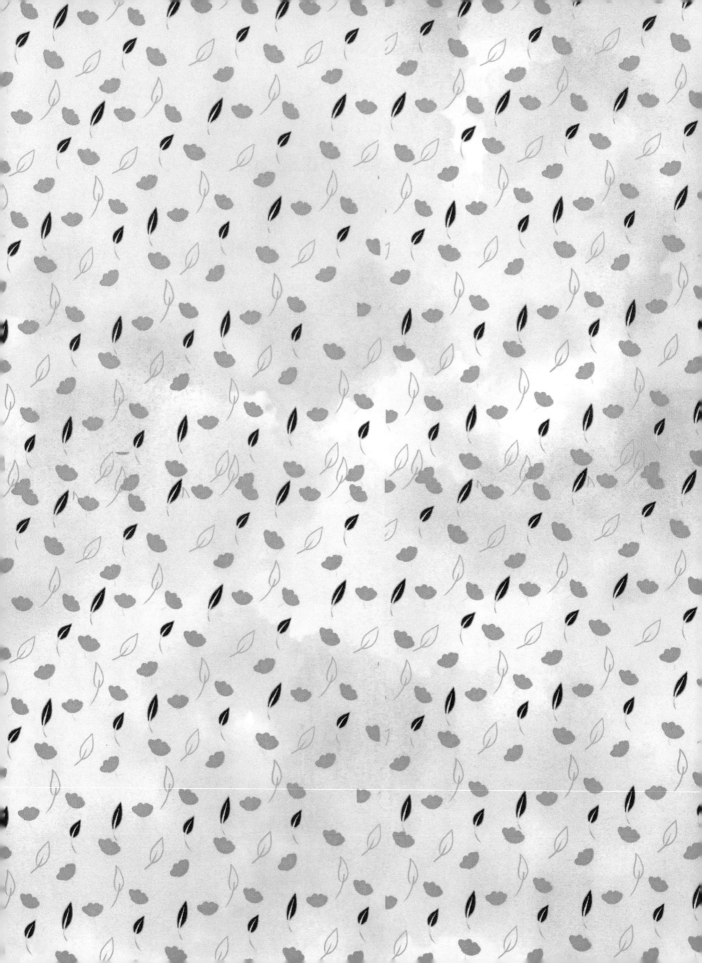

Made in the USA
Las Vegas, NV
13 December 2023

82742972R00017